GUN CAMERA
– WORLD WAR II

PHOTOGRAPHY FROM ALLIED FIGHTERS AND BOMBERS OVER OCCUPIED EUROPE

L. DOUGLAS KEENEY

MBI Publishing Company

This edition first published in 2000 by MBI Publishing Company,
729 Prospect Avenue, PO Box 1, Osceola, WI 54020-0001 USA.

Previously published by Avion Park, LLC Publishing.

MBI Publishing Company books are also available at discounts in
bulk quantity for industrial or sales-promotional use. For details
write to Special Sales Manager at Motorbooks International
Wholesalers & Distributors, 729 Prospect Avenue,
PO Box 1, Osceola, WI 54020-0001 USA.

Library of Congress Cataloging-in-Publication Data available

ISBN 0-7603-1013-0

Printed in China

pite the obvious risks, World War II was
[us]ually well covered by military and civil-
[ia]n photographers. They landed on D-Day,
[t]hey marched with the soldiers, they sailed
[w]ith the sailors —and they flew with the
[b]ombers over Nazi Germany. Images col-
lected by these "professionals" were taken
during real missions, and while the photographs tend to be reasonably sharp, the com-
positions look hurried. They were. There
was precious little time to compose a shot
when the plane beside you burst into flames.

A second type of photography in this book
is technically called GASP footage—an
acronym for Gun Alignment and Sighting
Photography, meaning gun camera footage.
[S]uch photography came from the smaller
[f]ighter planes and was taken by automatic
[ca]meras, almost all of it in bursts of just a
[f]ew seconds in length.

This book contains one of the most com-
prehensive collections of images from the
air war over occupied Europe and Nazi Germany ever published. Altogether, they form
a pictorial essay of World War II that you
will not soon forget.

ABOUT THE PHOTOGRAPHS

(Above) Four P-51 Mustangs return from a mission and pull up into a victory roll indicating wins over the Germans. A P-51 in the foreground is painted with the distinctive black-and-white pattern of D-Day to identify it as an Allied aircraft. This pattern came to be known as "invasion stripes."

INTRODUCTION

This is a picture of the air war in the European Theatre of World War II the way the pilots saw it. From the cockpit. From the waist gun slots. From P-51s chasing Bf-109s and from B-17s struggling to stay in formation and get home in one piece.

It is not a romantic picture, but neither was the war. It is, however, a vivid picture, told one flight at a time, one plane at a time, one day at a time, one personal triumph or tragedy at a time, for this is indeed the way wars are fought. Just ask any airman who was there.

No attempt has been made to trace the development of the Army Air Corps from an empty shell to 300,000 aircraft—nor has any effort been made to track the chronology of the air campaigns between 1939 and 1945. That history has been told in any number of fine books, most of which are readily available at local libraries and bookstores. The time period of this book spans the period between the first 8th Air Force mission in July, 1942 and the last in May of 1945. It begins with the bomber streams, continues with air-to-air dogfighting and ends with the dramatic use of fighters in the air-to-ground role.

The images assembled here are at once dramatic, stunning and oftentimes heart breaking. Many have never been published before. They tell a story about air war that words alone could not convey. About the sudden violence of an artillery shell that slams into the nose of a bomber or the prolonged terror of an aircrew struggling to climb out as they spiral 15,000 feet down towards the ground. About the seemingly random nature of death and survival as anti-aircraft fire picks apart a formation. About the practiced skill of a fighter pilot going air-to-air against a battle-hardened

Air crews preparing for the difficult missions over Hitler-held Europe well understood the gravity of such an undertaking. The Führer had amassed a superior air defense, and despite growing confidence, every man knew that each mission may be his last. Acknowledging a higher Presence in the violent skies over Europe, Captain James A. Burris, a Chaplain somewhere in the ETO, leads the crew of the "Lonesome Polecat" in prayer just prior to saddling-up.

enemy, some already with 300 victories in the sky.

While three types of missions are covered in this volume—air strikes, air-to-air dog-fighting and air-to-ground attack—one overall theme emerges, that of loneliness and isolation. In one photograph we see a single B-17 drop out of formation and fall in a sickening arc towards the ground 30,000 feet below. Around it, the bomber formation continues toward the target as if nothing has happened at all. But something has happened, and it is terrible indeed. One is immediately sickened to think of the frantic struggle that must be going on aboard that solo bomber. Lonely indeed.

For all of World War II, ETO and Pacific, 299,293 aircraft were built between 1940 and 1945. In that same period, 193,440 pilots were trained to fly along with 400,000 bombardiers, navigators, gunners and flight engineers. All told, 1,449 planes were lost per month during WWII—a total of 65,200 for the war. In turn, there were 120,000 Army Air Force casualties.

"We won't do much talking until we've done more fighting. After we're gone, we hope you'll be glad we came." General Ira Eaker said to the British public as he took command of the 8th Air Force in 1942.

Three years later the war would be won. Eaker and the men who flew the planes you will see on the following pages did the fighting—fighting for which the world is, indeed, eternally glad.

Before smart bombs, air superiority depended on the dead-eye accuracy and timing of well-drilled bombardiers like Lieutenant Samuel M. Slaton below. At well over five miles above his target, Lt. Slaton signals to his navigator, "mission accomplished." And yet the toughest part of their mission lay ahead—that of returning their Flying Fortress safely to base amid the roving fire of Luftwaffe aces and the deadly flak that blossomed in the skies over Europe.

(Left) A B-17 Flying Fortress. The Fort was one of the principal bombers in the strategic air campaign against Germany.

(Left) A lone P-38 stands guard over the invasion beaches of Normandy just days after D-Day. The Lightning was called "the forked-tail devil" by the Germans not just because of its deadly speed or its superior agility, which it had, but because it was such an over-powering air-to-air fighter.

THE BOMBERS

Bomber streams make their way over Germany and as they do, they are met by intense flak and German fighters. (Left) Seen here from the ball turret of a B-17 (notice the vertical stabilizer—the tail—to the far right), black puffs of deadly steel lace the sky. In the lower right, a B-17 falls away from the formation after a direct hit. German artillery was deadly accurate and although the bombers were remarkably rugged, 17,432 were lost to the ack-ack fire.

Engine out and smoking, the crew of this B-17 will be forced to bail out.

A German rocket reaches up toward a B-17, narrowly missing the wing, but exploding nonetheless between the two engines on the left side. The photograph has captured the shell as it detonates, but not the reaction of the bomber to the inevitable spray of shrapnel and the concussive force of the proximity explosion. Bomber crews suffered from the anxiety of not knowing when an anti-aircraft shell would find its mark—a terrible stress magnified evermore because they couldn't see the shells coming up.

(Right) The tail gunner blazes away with his twin, 50 cal. guns as German fighters sweep in on this B-17. The B-17 could pour tremendous firepower into the sky—ten barrels bristle from the bomber. Notice the damage already sustained to the bomber's right wing. While this bomber appears to be flying straight-and-level, the pilot is actually struggling to bring it home and thus avoid bailing out over enemy territory. The typical crew complement on a B-17 was ten. All of them carried the rank of sergeant or higher as the Germans tended to treat NCOs and officers better than they did privates.

(Below) Waist gunners of the 91st bomb group prepare to defend their B-17 from assaults by the agile German foe. The B-17's numerous defensible positions from nose to tail indeed made it a "Flying Fortress". Notice the waist gunner's post just above and to the right of the star and bars in the image at right.

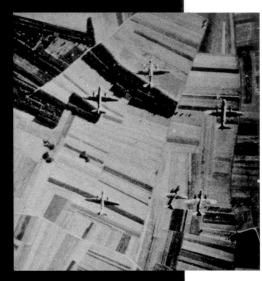
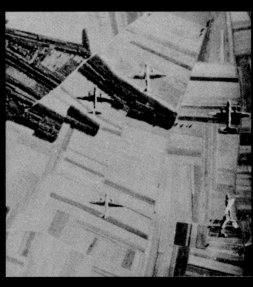

This unusual sequence of shots captures an accident that has rarely been seen on film. These A-20s have just released bombs—one of which hits the trailing plane in the center. Spinning out of control to the right, it heads directly toward a second plane in the formation and despite efforts to get out of the way, they collide. The second bomber is chopped in half and both crash to the ground. During the war, B-17s and B-24s were also bombed by their own formations.

The Germans threw
everything they could think
of at the bombers. In
addition to flak and fighters,
they developed air-to-air
"mortar" shells that could
be fired into a formation
from a half mile away. They
also tried "bombing" the
formations from above with
their own bombers. As crazy
as it sounds, crews were lost
to these desperate tactics.

In this picture, flak comes up
to meet a 1,000-plane
bomber stream attacking
Berlin on March 22, 1945.
Fighter opposition was light.
The B-17 at the top has been
hit and has an engine on fire.
Owing to turbochargers, the
B-17 could fly as high as
35,000 feet thus avoiding
some ground fire.

(Right) A waist gunner leans into the slipstream to look for targets while the ball turret underneath him fires straight down on an attacking Bf-109.

(Below) Under attack by an Me-110, these B-17s of the 91st Bomb Group rely on the strength of a tightly packed formation to bring as much defensive firepower as possible to bear on the attacking Germans. As cruel as it may seem, pilots stayed in formation even as other bombers dropped away and became easy prey for the attacking fighters. Fifty bombers meant five hundred guns. It was safer in the packs.

This B-17 has suffered a direct hit during a mission over the rail yards in Budapest. Five crew members bailed out before the bomber crashed. Notice the cavity in the fuselage, now a 200 mile-per-hour wind tunnel.

Anti-aircraft fire finds a target twice. (Right) All that remains of this B-17 is a cloud of black smoke and the fire of four burning engines after the Germans score a direct hit. This Fortress was part of Operation Titanic, the codename for the "shuttle" bombing missions flown between bases in England and Russia.

(Below) An A-20 takes a direct hit in the tail by AA fire. Notice the fragments flying through the air above the bomber. Photographed from the bomber below it in formation, the Havoc crashed immediately after this photo was taken.

(Left) A B-24 spins down toward occupied France after taking a hit by German anti-aircraft fire. (Below) This B-17 has suffered a direct hit and has broken into three pieces— the tail, seen in the upper left corner of the photo, the mid-section to the right and the forward section, upside down, toward the bottom of the picture. Other aircrews in the formation will anxiously watch a bomber for parachutes. Once they got a clean chute, the riskiest part of their bailout was the moment they landed on the ground. Irate German farmers were more likely to attack and kill them than were German soldiers. All told, 11,567 airmen were held in POW camps following bailouts.

An A-26 Invader spins out of control after a direct hit to its left wing during a bombing run. Notice the opened bomb bay doors.

Tail-damaged, this B-24 continues on to the target.

Heroically, but vainly, the pilot of this B-26 is applying full right aileron in an attempt to maintain control but the flak damage is too much and the opposing lift flips the bomber onto its back. It crashed. No chutes were seen.

The B-17 could take an incredible punishment. The tail of this Fortress was shot away over Italy and yet the pilot was able to wrestle her home. When it was hit, the tail gunner was blown out of the plane but he got a clean chute.

The nose of this bomber has been blown off by a direct hit from a German 88 mm shell. Miraculously, the pilot survived and was able to fly the plane back to its home base and give the crew time to safely bail out over friendly territory. The bombardier and navigator were killed instantly.

BAIL-OUTS

During World War II there were only two ways to get out of a plane. You climbed out. Or you fell out. Ejection seats were years away. In the fighters, some pilots turned their planes upside-down and then released their shoulder harnesses and fell away. Others preferred to climb out on the side and jump. In bombers, the crew had to make it to the nearest escape hatch. Because this took time, pilots would struggle to keep their aircraft steady until everyone was out.

Burning, but still in formation, not much time remains for this B-24 Liberator. Hit by anti-aircraft fire, the bomber ultimately broke into two and crashed, but in this incredible shot, you can actually see a crewman pushing his way through the top escape hatch. This is just behind the cockpit and forward of the gun turret. As the B-24 crashed, bombers in the formation reported seeing "many" chutes. The B-24 typically had a crew of ten.

(Left) Perhaps one of the most chilling photographs to come out of the air war was this one—a B-17 tumbling to the ground, her wing torn off at the root, the airplane blasted upside down by the concussive force of exploding flak. Five parachutes were seen. Used in books, on posters and included in many histories of the war, this is how the original print looks.

(Below) A B-17 is hit in the #3 engine and falls out of formation and into an uncontrollable spin. It will crash onto the streets of Berlin.

This B-24 Liberator is actually rolling over onto its back. The left wing has collapsed at the outboard engine mount and the right wing, which is generating almost all of the lift, is rolling the plane over. Many times pilots flew unflyable airplanes—airplanes with half a wing shot away, for example—and miraculously got their crews home, but recovery from a rolling spin such as this was unlikely.

The last moments of this Liberator are at hand. Although she continues straight-and-level with all four engines dutifully flying the plane, fire has engulfed the bomber and the end is near. No one wanted to think what horrors were unfolding inside her burning hull. With profound feelings of despair and helplessness, other planes would ease away from the burning bomber least they get hit by the inevitable explosion. While the British flew at night and flew as singles, the Americans bombed during the day and flew in packs. Watching one's buddies die was an unbearable consequence of daylight bombing.

Moments after this picture was taken, this B-24 lost its left wing. Nine parachutes were seen opening.

This B-17 was hit on July 5, 1944 during a mission over Hungary.

The Douglas A-20 was a fast, medium bomber with a crew of three. A total of 7,385 were built. In this picture, flak has scored a hit, igniting first the fuel lines then the main fuel tanks. This was taken somewhere over Nazi Germany during a low-level attack.

With puffy white clouds silhouetting this unspeakable violence, a B-24 Liberator has been blown into two by a clean hit from an artillery shell. The resulting image has an almost surreal quality to it.

(Left) A particularly striking photograph from the air war. During a mission over southern France, a B-26 Marauder takes a direct hit to its right engine, which can be seen falling away at the bottom of the picture, the prop still spinning. Severed hydraulics probably account for the release of the landing gear housed behind the engine. The pilot was unable to regain control of the plane and crashed moments after this picture was taken.

This B-24 was hit on September 7, 1944 during a raid on German installations in Austria. German fighter resistance was fierce, downing all of the attacking Liberators except for the one from which this photograph was taken.

(Right) A lone B-17 is chased to the ground by a German FW-190.

A Nazi fighter is seen in the background of this photo as it begins its attack on a B-17 of the 100th Bomb Group. In attacking bombers, the Germans would try to get a kill from the very outer limits of their guns and thus avoid the kill radius of the defensive fire of the American guns.

(This page, top) A B-24 burns after breaking apart on landing. The crew escaped.

(Below) The wounded are carried off a B-17.

(Right) A B-17 has crash landed and burned in the fields of France. The crew escaped. Notice the zig-zagging German bunkers and the tunnels. American soldiers encountered these defenses as they drove from Aachen to Berlin.

As the faces of this returning bomber crew attest, there was no real joy returning from a mission— there was only survival.

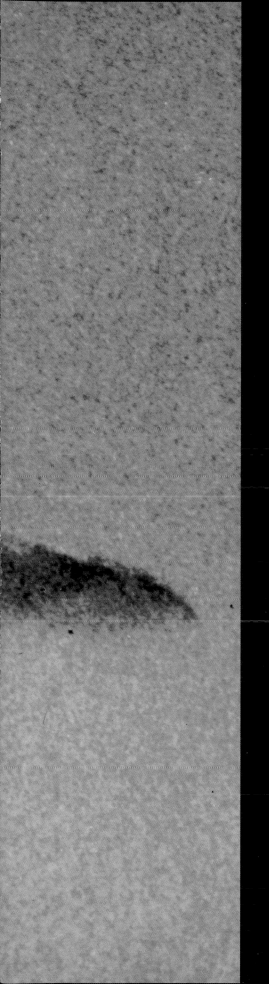

AIR TO AIR

Nothing surprised the Luftwaffe more than to discover that American fighter pilots could actually shoot them down in a dogfight. After all, the Germans were battle-hardened and had victories over both the British and the Soviets. Indeed, some of their top pilots had 300 aerial kills. "Who are these inexperienced farm boys fighting in the skies?" they would ask.

Farm boys indeed. In the years since World War II, the Air Force has tried to answer that exact question themselves. What *had* made their pilots so good? As it happened, not much. Patriotism, to be sure. A sense of duty, no doubt. But beyond that, two ordinary traits rose above all others—that they *were* simple farm boys, and that they had experience with a rifle. Squirrel-hunting farm boys processed through a good training program married to good planes like the P-51 Mustang, the P-38 Lightning and the P-47 Thunderbolt could kill German airplanes. This combination of simple traits—that, and an overpowering sense of duty— would lead to Allied dominance of the skies over Germany. As Eisenhower would say, Hitler was about to "feel the fury of an aroused Democracy".

Feel it he did.

(Left) A P-38 Lightning tucks in alongside a stream of B-17s.

They were called "little friends". The P-51, P-38 and the P-47 fighters that escorted

the bomber streams as they flew deep into German territory. A most welcome sight

indeed, the little friends had a straightforward job—to protect the bombers. Straight-

forward, yes, but it was hard duty. In the early years, they could only go so far. At

some point in every mission, the little friends would rock their wings, whisper a

prayer and turn back, leaving the B-17s and B-24s to their own defenses, alone over

German territory. It was disheartening to say the least and the bombers would

inevitably be ravaged by the waiting Germans. Thankfully, along came two

remedies. Better drop tanks. And the P-51 Mustang. Together, fighters now had the

range to escort their bombers all the way into Berlin and back home again.

(Facing page, and this page). Puffs of flak dot the skies. German fighters dart about a formation of attacking B-17s. One B-17 falls away, its tail section blown off. Seen in these photos, the lone B-17 flutters down in a slow spin. No chutes were reported.

During a mission over Bremen, Germany, a Focke-Wolf 190 attacks a B-17. This was photographed from a bomber just ahead in the formation.

(Left and above) An Me-110 is the target of two P-47 Thunderbolts. Engaged in a classic tail chase, the first P-47 records hits on the German's right wing before he is cut off by a second P-47 and is forced to cease firing. The second P-47 finishes off the 110. In the excitement of the chase, the second Thunderbolt might not have seen the first. In the early stages of the air war, American fighter pilots could only engage the Germans when they attacked a formation. As time passed, that changed, and American pilots would be free to hunt the Germans down.

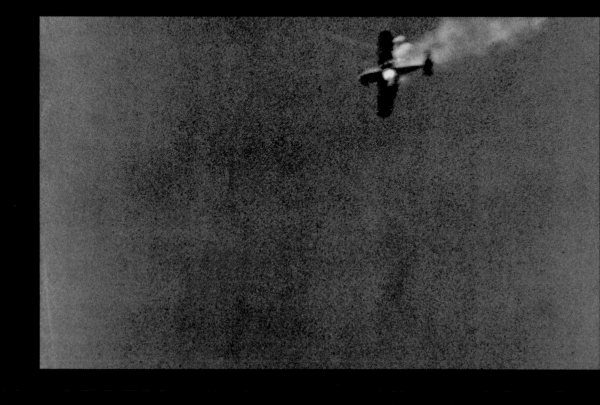

An air-to-air dogfight ends with another American victory. (Left) Notice the pilot bailing out during this sequence. He emerges from the airplane in the picture at the top and falls away in the two photos just below.

(This page and facing page) This four-shot sequence from the gun cameras of a P-47 records the explosive mid-air destruction of a German Focke-Wulf. This dogfight came to an end less than 100 feet above the ground. The angle of the photo and the proximity to the ground is confusing—the blast looks more like an ammunition dump exploding than a fighter plane coming apart.

Hits register as bright flashes along the wing and fuselage of this FW-190 over Germany.

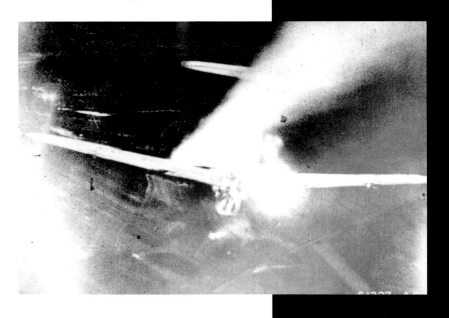

(Three photos) In a near vertical dive through the clouds, this Bf-109 is killed by the pilot of a P-51. The German fighters were supposed to avoid dogfighting and instead attack the bomber formations.

(Below and right) The angles in these pictures are deceptive. This Bf-109-F is actually inverted and diving down for the deck. He is being chased by a P-51 Mustang. The effort is in vain, however, as bullets find their mark. In the picture to the right, the American pilot has purposely eased back to avoid the debris as his target explodes.

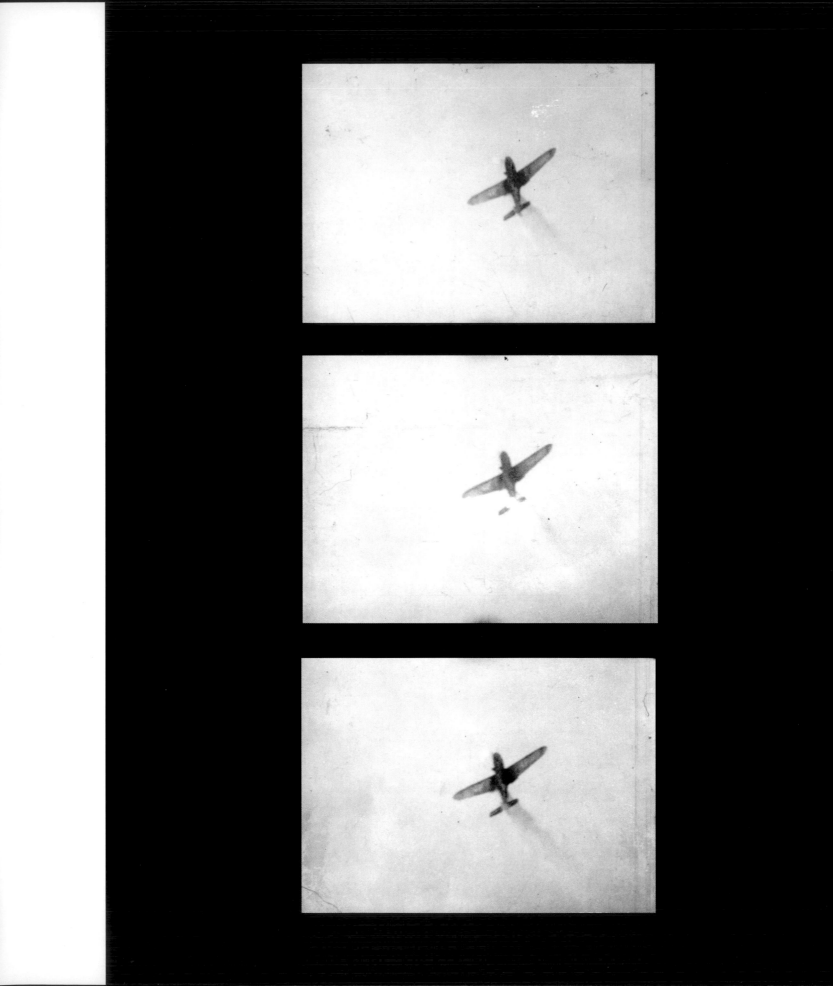

The pilot of this Bf-109 has bailed out even though his plane seems relatively intact. Although it was more the exception than the rule, some of the less experienced German pilots would jump as soon as they were attacked by an American.

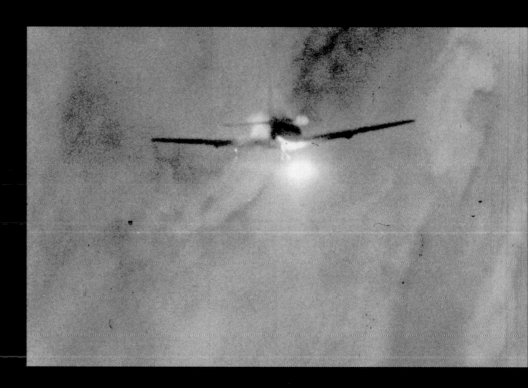

Twisting, turning and upside down, a pilot did every-

thing possible to stay on the tail of his opponent. Ver-

tigo would seem to have been a problem, but it was

not. What concerned the pilots most was the danger of

building up too much speed in a dive and pulling the

wings off.

(Above and facing page) Against the backdrop of the snow covered Ardennes, a P-51 tail-chases a Bf-109. The large object on the plane's belly is a drop tank. The object seen coming off the fighter in the photo to the right is a piece of the engine cowling. This dogfight took place in January, 1945.

B-60289 A.C.

An FW-190 (above) and a Bf-109 (right) caught by 8th Air Force fighters on November 11, 1943.

Shells strike the cowling of a Bf-109. This engagement was credited as a kill.

Flashes on the wing skin of a Bf-109 as it is hit by the guns of a P-47

A Junkers Ju-88 hit on February 16, 1943

172

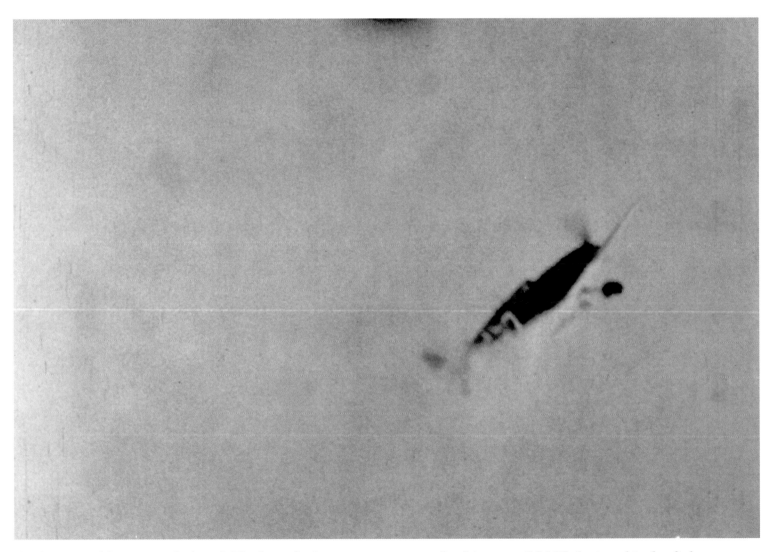

(Left, top and bottom and above) Flashes of white register as gun fire hits on a Bf-109 during this dogfight sequence shot by an American fighter pilot engaged in battle over Germany.

(Left and above) The final moments in a dogfight are seen on these two pages. Already streaming smoke, one more burst from a P-47 completes the kill. The P-47 was armed with eight .50 caliber guns—four to a wing—and while better known for its superb air-to-ground capabilities, it was also well-loved by its pilots as a dogfighter.

(Right) A Bf-109 is shot down during a low-level dogfight over Germany. Virtually every fighter pilot knew that blending in with the ground clutter was one way to shake a plane off his tail. It wasn't a guarantee, as this sequence clearly demonstrates, but it did work.

An Me-110 just a few yards in front of the gun camera.

1

2

3

50916 A.C.

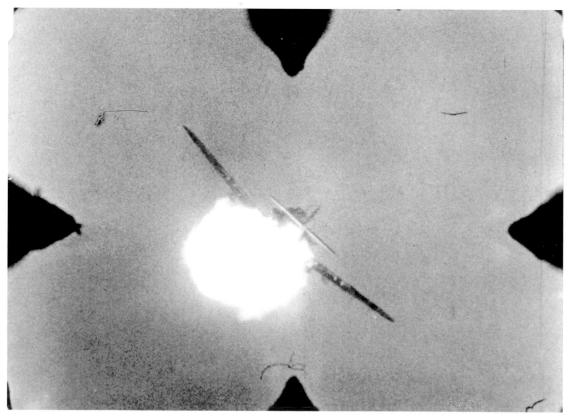

(Left, top and bottom, and above) This three picture gun camera sequence shows a German FW-190 caught by a P-47. The violent explosion results from the drop tank igniting. The German crash landed in the snowy fields below. Both the Americans and the Germans would ordinarily pickle their drop tanks before a fight, not only to improve their agility but to prevent something like this from happening.

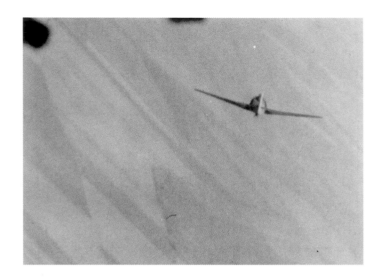 

Following an intense air-to-air dogfight, the pilot of this Nazi fighter begins to push himself out of the cockpit and bail out. In the picture above you can see his head and upper torso emerging from the cockpit. The full bailout can be seen in the photos on the facing page.

The German pilot pushes himself out of his cockpit, narrowly missing the horizontal stabilizer.

His hand on his parachute chord, the pilot starts to recover from the bail-out and begins to pull the handle.

This remarkably clear photo sequence apparently conveyed a sense of power that was particularly appealing to the Secretary of the Army Air Corps. During the summer of 1944, he used these photographs to illustrate a then-secret report prepared for the Secretary of War. Showing a perfectly executed tail chase, the Nazi fighter is lined up by the American pilot (below) and then hit in the engine by a burst (facing page, top). Spewing smoke (facing page, bottom), the Nazi plane spins into the ground. The gear has fallen (facing page, bottom) due to the loss of hydraulic fluids. Also notice the empty hard point along the centerline. This would have held the drop tank.

(Right) Two circles help untangle this picture. In the circle to the left is an American P-51. At the right is a German Me-110. This dogfight has come down to within a few feet of the treetops. The P-51 has stayed with the fight to insure the kill even though the Me-110 is already on fire. (Below) An Me-109 is hit by the deadly accurate fire of a P-47.

An Me-163 pitches over into an inverted spin after the pilot of a P-47 lands hits on its tail.
Hitler hoped his new jet technologies would reverse the course of the war and jet planes were
the cornerstone to that plan. Vastly superior performance made the Me-163 a potentially
deadly air-to-air adversary but it came into the war too late to do any good. The twin-engine
version, the Me-262, was actually produced in some quantity—over 1,000 in all—but only a
few hundred entered service. The rest were destroyed by the Allies.

55773 A C

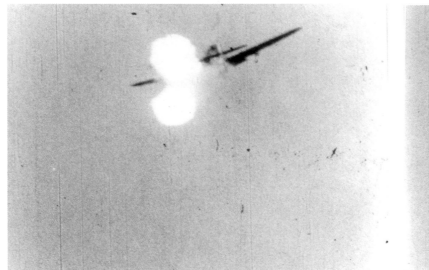

Gun camera footage of an FW-190. The official Army Air Corps name for gun camera footage was actually "GASP" footage meaning Gun Alignment and Sighting Photography, although it was never called that by the pilots.

(Right, three photos) A Junkers JU-88 in a tail chase over Germany shortly before D-Day. American fighters increased their mission cycles leading up to the June 6th invasion to prevent the Nazis from using their air assets against the landing forces on the Normandy beaches. Following the invasion, the Germans largely conceded the air space over southern France and instead concentrated their forces in the north, to stop the deadly bomber streams.

 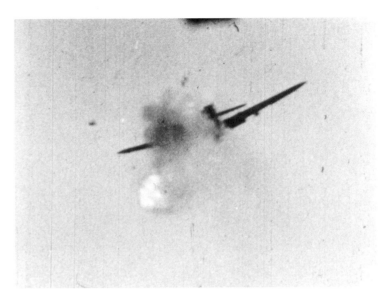

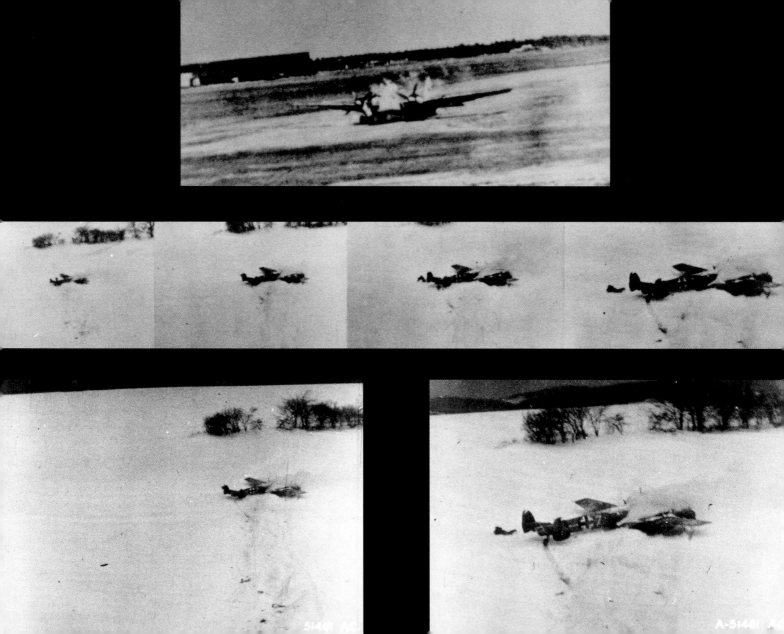

(Facing page) In the end, this is what the American bomber pilots wanted to see— German airplanes being destroyed. On the left, top, an He-111 takes hits as it sits on the ramp at a German airfield. Below that, a sequence strip from gun camera films shows an Me-110 after it has crashed. In the right frame, you can see the pilot sprawled out on the ground. Caught between a plane that might explode and the gun fire around him, the Nazi pilot burrows into the ground. American pilots rarely attacked Luftwaffe pilots once their planes crashed. There was no hesitation, however, about destroying the downed aircraft.

P-47s were called into action to support the American divisions as they advanced through Germany. This Thunderbolt suffered a direct hit on the left wing while pummeling a column of Nazi tanks in cooperation with the 12th Armored Division's attack. Realizing the danger he posed to friendly troops below, the pilot chose to ride the plane into the ground rather than bail out. He emerged from the wreckage near Wurtsburg, Germany with only minor injuries.

In this rare photograph, a young German pilot ruefully inspects the wreckage of his plane with men from the 90th Division, a group whose anti-aircraft fire was responsible for eight other "kills" that same day. A .50 caliber bullet found the magneto on his Bf-109, forcing him out of the skies over Halstroff, France. As German air superiority became seriously compromised in 1944, younger pilots were enlisted to fill the shoes of the legendary Luftwaffe flyers who came before them.

In this photo, ground crewmen scramble to pull an unconscious pilot from his flak-riddled P-47 in France. Notice the shredded skin of his left wing—a testimonial to the hell-fire rained on Allied fighters by Nazi airmen. The airstrip upon which he crashed was established and constructed in a matter of days after the invasion at Normandy—a credit to the resourceful engineers of our invasion forces. This swiftness was critical to success in the eventual liberation of France, allowing Allied fighter planes to keep the Luftwaffe at bay.

(This page) A German FW-190 is little more than twisted aluminum after being downed by American artillery fire. The body of the pilot smolders.

(Facing page) A well-placed machine gun blast can send an airplane to the ground like a leaden bird. This injured pilot escapes from the cockpit of his downed plane with the assistance of men from the 5th Armored Division, 9th U.S. Army in Germany.

No one liked the war. Even when a photographer asked them to smile for the folks back home, a smile was hard to find. (Below) The thrill of twenty-two aerial victories can't take away the tension in the face of Captain Fred J. Christensen, Jr., a twenty-two-year-old Massachusetts son photographed somewhere in France. Aces like Christensen knew the horror of dying in the gunsights of a fighter—he had shot down too many planes not to think about his own mortality. But for the will of God, they knew. But for the will of God.

AIR TO GROUND

While today it is ordinary battle doctrine, the use of fighter-bombers in the close air support role was a novel idea in 1944. Indeed, the D-Day invasion plans failed to include even a rudimentary communication loop between the ground forces and the air. Hastily rectified, the soldiers could soon radio for air strikes and within minutes expect to see fighters swooping in for pinpoint accurate bombing runs on the Germans. The P-47 Thunderbolt, seen here silhouetted in the explosion of an ammo dump, was the backbone of the close air support fighter fleet in Europe and was one of the most feared Allied assets in the drive across France and on to Berlin. The Germans nicknamed the ungainly fighter "Jabo".

In the beginning of the air war, the American escorts were never allowed to separate from the bombers to dive down and attack even the most obvious of ground targets. That changed as the Nazi air-to-air threat diminished. During the later stages of the air campaign, the doctrine was rewritten to require pilots to drop down and strafe targets of opportunity. Tough planes like the P-47 were ideal for air-to-ground combat. With eight .50 caliber machine guns and a five-hundred-pound bomb under each wing, their fire power and their accuracy were awesome. There were, of course, risks. The pilots knew that they would encounter everything from heavy anti-aircraft fire to deadly small arms. Nonetheless, hundreds of German planes were destroyed on the ground with relatively light Allied losses. Gun camera footage on these two pages shows a pilot flying multiple passes on the same field, a risky proposition at best. Most pilots attempted only one fast pass.

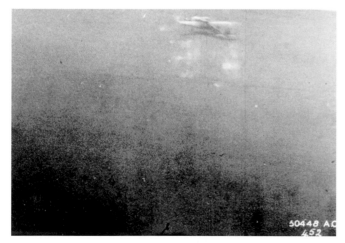 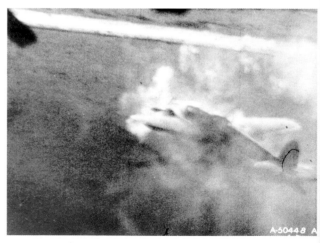

(Above) A P-47 sweeps down on a German airfield and riddles a parked aircraft with its .50 cal. fire.

(Preceding page) A P-47 is silhouetted by the explosion of an ammunition truck. Pilots got particular satisfaction from a good secondary but there were risks here too—flying debris and the blast concussion itself could down the attacking fighter. In this case, the Thunderbolt flew through the blast and safely returned to base.

(Above) Identified as an Me-210, the engines of this plane made deep ruts in a freshly plowed farm as it bellied in for a crash landing.

(Top) Bullets "walk" up toward a German plane. (Bottom) A P-47 down on the deck. In the motion picture footage of this sequence, the P-47 actually glances off the grass as he swoops in for the pass. Pilots made light of these ultra-low passes variously calling them "mowing the grass", "bunny sucking", or simply "flying with your hair on fire".

51036 A.C

A P-47 Thunderbolt swoops in low over an artillery observation tower. Seen from the vantage of his wingman, puffs of smoke and dust record hits as this Jug picks apart yet another target of opportunity.

(Above) A turn-around point on a canal somewhere in Nazi-occupied Europe. Air-to-ground attacks such as these made it impractical for the Nazis to plan major movements of troops or material during daylight hours. Nazi ground movement was relegated to the night.

(Facing page) 8th Air Force fighters sweep in over trains and trucks. Anything that moved was fair game.

Trains were marvelous targets of opportunity and were attacked vigorously. But, as with everything in war, nothing was as good as it seemed. The Nazis routinely used American or civilian prisoners to shield the rails. Worse, the boxcars were just as likely to be crammed with American POWs or civilians as ammunition or weapons. The ideal train was a flat rail car.

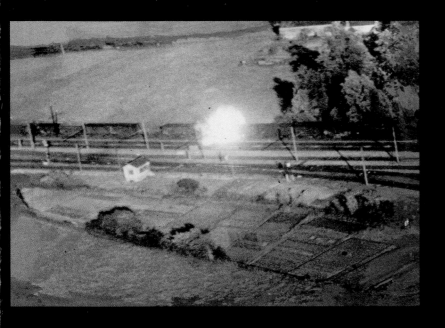

A strong secondary marks this air-to-ground attack. The intensity suggests a fuel depot. The 8th Air Force press office said that the fireball was so hot that it scorched the paint off the bottom of the fighter.

"To harrass, obstruct, disrupt and destroy enemy communications and the flow of supplies." These were the marching orders for the pilots flying the P-47s, P-51s and P-38s that roamed the skies of occupied Europe. Whether they were locating ammunition dumps behind an innocent farm house (right), or attacking trains (this page), the pilots used trial-and-error to devise the tactics for air-to-ground attack. Their tactics would become battle doctrine for generations of flyers to come.

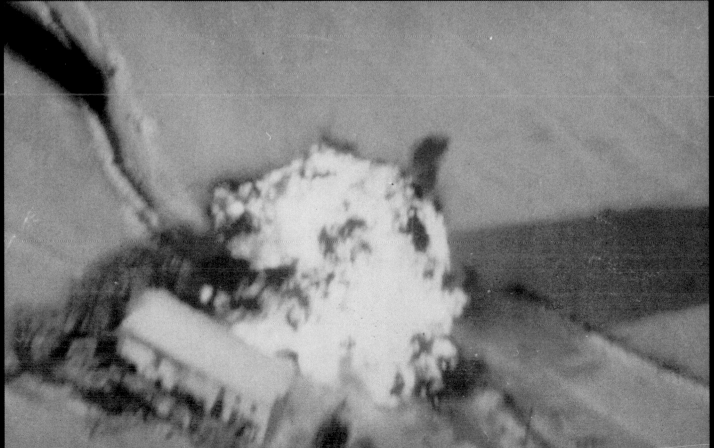

A bare airfield is attacked by Americans. Revetments and hangars were rare in the occupied countries but were a constant problem when attacking the home airfields in Germany.

126

(Clockwise from the upper left) A German airfield near Verdun is attacked (a JU-52, JU-88 and a Bf-109 are visible, left to right). An He-111 is strafed by a P-38, also at Verdun. Two views of an airfield near Brandenburg, Germany.

(Facing page) A P-38 strafes a train at Landsberg, Germany.

A P-47 makes a low pass over a German aerodrome while his wingman shoots up a Potez-63. Notice the fuel leaking from bullet holes in the Nazi aircraft's right wing.

EPILOGUE

Most of my friends know of my interest in World War II history, and because of that, they almost always bring up the war and say how timeless it seems to be or how clear it was, back then, who was good and who was evil. In these respects, they are correct. World War II does have a timeless quality to it, waxing and waning in popularity, yes, but always there, always of interest, always a story worth telling and retelling yet again. It is also true that the lines between good and evil were clearly drawn. One can say without fear of revisionism, that the Allies stood for freedom while the Axis powers were the oppressors.

Simplifying World War II, however, can be a dangerous thing. What is often forgotten in the din of cocktail conversation is that World War II was a terrible, terrible thing. This was drilled home to me in a particularly embarassing exchange with one of our greatest air aces. I must have said something that bordered on the notion that the men who fought in WWII were brave heroes and that dashing into the air to fight the Nazis was somehow glamorous. In the sternest language possible, I was reminded that this was absolutely untrue. The war was hell and fighting was a matter of duty, not glory. Living conditions were terrible, meals were cold, and there were many days with long hours doing absolutely nothing. Then there were the missions, and the constant prospect of being trapped in a burning B-17 or killed by bullets slamming into your P-51. They'd all seen it happen—seen their friends push out of a fighter only to fall thousands of feet to their deaths when a parachute failed to blossom, or helped pull a buddy out of a bomber with an eye shot out or a leg chewed up by shrapnel.

This war was not about glamour or heroics but, rather, about duty. Men fought because it was their duty to fight, and because they lived up to this obligation, the war was won. In the end, getting home was all that they really wanted and, to that end, they would fly just about any mission. They never thought about medals or ribbons or parades. They simply wanted to get back home.

Today, we are a free world because of this enormous sacrifice. This book is dedicated to the men who fought the air war over Europe.

—L.D.K